Out in the weather

Jenny Giles

Illustrated by Betty Greenhatch

D1796052

It is a rainy day.

Look at us.

It is a cloudy day.

Look at us.

It is a windy day.

Look at us.

It is a frosty day.

Look at us.

It is a snowy day.

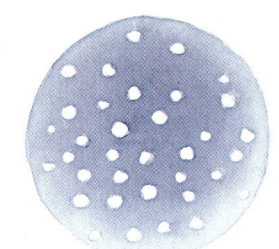

Look at us.

It is a stormy day.

Look at us.

It is a sunny day ...

15

Look at us!